Configuration of Microsoft ISA Proxy Server and Linux Squid Proxy Server

By
Dr. Hidaia Mahmood Alassouli

1. OVERVIEW

The paper concerns about basic Microsoft ISA server and Linux Squid Server configuration As a lot of technicians switch between ISA server and Squid server, I decided to write this paper to present some reference when configuring ISA and Squid. There a lot of issues that not covered, and you can go to the manual of ISA server and Squid server for detailed configuration of ISA and Squid. The paper is composed from two parts
1. Microsoft ISA server 2004 Configuration
2. Linux Squid Server Configuration

Note that, this work was done without proper simulation, because of the lack of resources, as testing firewall configuration requires many computers, with one of them should have many network cards. Also the ISA server is not used in the computer center now.

KEYWORDS:
Internet Security Acceleration Server, ISA Server, Squid Server, Proxy, Firewall.

2. MICROSOFT ISA SERVER 2004

2.1 MAIN OPERATION:

All of the network rules and access rules make up the firewall policy. The firewall policy is applied in the following way:

1. A user using a client computer sends a request for a resource located on the Internet.

2. If the request comes from a Firewall Client computer, the user is transparently authenticated using Kerberos or NTLM if domain authentication is configured. If the user cannot be transparently authenticated, ISA Server requests the user credentials. If the user request comes from a Web proxy client, and the access rule requires authentication, ISA Server requests the user credentials. If the user request comes from a SecureNAT client, the user is not authenticated, but all other network and access rules are still applied.

3. ISA Server checks the network rules to verify that the two networks are connected. If no network relationship is defined between the two networks,
the request is refused.

4. If the network rules define a connection between the source and destination networks, ISA Server processes the access rules. The rules are applied in order of priority as listed in the ISA Server Management interface. If an allow rule allows the request, then the request is forwarded without checking any additional access rules. If no access rule allows the request, the final default access rule is applied, which denies all access.

5. If the request is allowed by an access rule, ISA Server checks the network rules again to determine how the networks are connected. ISA Server checks the Web chaining rules (if a Web proxy client requested the object) or the firewall chaining configuration (if a SecureNAT or Firewall Client requested the object) to determine how the request will be serviced.

6. The request is forwarded to the Internet Web server.

2.2 TYPE OF NETWORKS AND NETWORK RELATIONSHIPS AND ISA SERVER CLIENTS:

The default type of networks,
- **VPN Clients-** Built-in dynamic network object representing client computers connected to ISA Server via VPN.
- **Internal-** Network representing the internal network, i.e. 10.12.00.00 -10.12.255.254.
- **Local Host-** Built-in network object representing the ISA Server computer
- **Quarantined VPN Clients-** Built-in dynamic network representing client computers connecting to ISA Server via VPN that are currently quarantined.
- **Perimeter-** Network object representing a perimeter network (also known as DMZ, demilitarized zone, and screened subnet).
- **External-** Network object representing the Internet.

There are two types of network relationships:
a) **Route:** ISA server routes traffic between network sources and destinations (no network translations is used). Routed relationships is directional.
b) **NAT:** ASA server hides the source computers by replacing their network IP address of its outgoing traffic by its external IP address.

ISA Server provides secure access to internet for all of its clients. ISA server has three type of clients:
- **Firewall clients:** Firewall clients are computers that have firewall client software installed and enabled. When computer with firewall client software installed makes a request for resources on internet, the request is directed to firewall service on ISA server computer. The firewall service will authenticate and authorize the user and filter the request based on firewall rules and application filters and other add-ins. The Firewall service may also cache the requested object or serve the object from the ISA server cache using web proxy filter. Firewall clients provide highest level of functionality.
- **SecureNAT clients:** SecureNAT clients are computers that don't have firewall client installed. Instead, SecureNAT clients are configured to route all requests for resources on other networks to an internal IP address on the computer running ISA server. If the network includes only a single segment, the SecureNAT client is configured to use the internal IP address on the computer running ISA server as the default gateway. Requests from SecureNAT clients are directed first to the network address translation (NAT) driver, which substitutes the ISA server external IP address for the internal IP address of the SecureNAT client. The client request is then directed to firewall service to determine if the access is allowed. Finally, the request maybe filtered by application filters and other extensions. The firewall service may cache the request object or deliver the object to ISA server cache. You need to configure only the default gateway of the client computers.
- **Web Proxy Clients:** They are any computers that run CERN-compatible web application such as web browsers. Requests from the web proxy clients are directed to firewall service on the ISA server computer to determine if the access is allowed. The firewall

service may also cache the requested object or serve the object from the ISA server web cache. The web application must be configured to use the ISA server.

2.3. CONFIGURING THE ISA SERVER AS PROXY AND FIREWALL:

All the HTTP requests pass through the web proxy component on ISA server, regardless of the client type. To configure the ISA server as proxy, expand the Configuration, and then Networks, and click the network whose web access properties you would like to configure, this is usually the internal network. Click Edit the selected Network, and in the Web Proxy Tab, ensure that Enable Web Proxy Clients is selected, and you can configure in this tab the following:
- Enable HTTP: Configure the ISA Server to listen on the HTTP connections on specified port, i.e. 80 or 8080
- Enable SSL: Configures ISA server to listen on for HTTPS connections on specified port number. If you enable SSL, you must also configure a Certificate that will be used for SSL authentication and encryption. Web browsers cant use this setting but can be used for web chaining.
- Authentication method: Configure methods of authentication supported by ISA server.
- Requires all users to authenticate: Configure ISA server to allow only authenticated users to access other networks. If you choose this option, SecureNAT will not be able to access the internet using ISA server.
- Authentication domain: Configure the default domain that will be used for authentication when using Basic, Digest, or Remote Authentication Dial-In User service (RADIUS) authentication.
- Number of connections: Configure the number of users that can connect to ISA server at one time.
- Connection timeout: Configures the connection timeout for idle connections.

In Firewall Client Tab, ensure that Enable Firewall client support for this network is selected, and use a Web proxy server is selected, and configure the ISA server name or IP address.

2.4. MAIN TYPES OF NETWORK TEMPLATES:

The best starting point for the firewall configuration is to see the rule base constructed automatically for the ISA 2004 server templates.

2.4.1. SINGLE NETWORK ADAPTER:

Specify that the ISA server will be used in a single network adapter configuration inside your internal or perimeter network In this case the ISA server will be used for web proxying, caching, Web publishing and OWA server publishing. The ISA server cant be used as edge firewall, and will not support IP-level and transport level packet filtering, VPN, server publishing and Firewall clients.

I. Apply default web proxing and cache configuration:
Creates a default rule, denying access to all networks. You can subsequently configure firewall policy rules to allow Web clients to access Web content on the Internet and configure caching to accelerate Web performance. Use this option when a single network adapter is installed on your ISA Server computer. The rule base created by default

Rule Name	From	To	Protocol	Network Relation	Users	Action
Local Host Access	Local host	All networks		Route		
VPN Clients to Internal Network	Quarantined VPN Clients, VPN Clients	Internal		Route		
Internet Access	Quarantined VPN Clients, VPN Clients, Internal	External		NAT		
Default Rule	All Networks	All Networks	All Traffic		All	Reject

2.4.2. EDGE FIREWALL TEMPLATE:

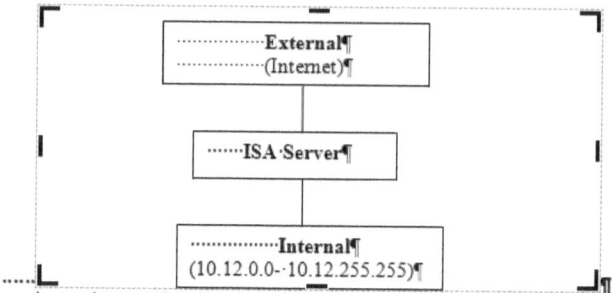

Connect your internal network to internet and protect it from intruders.

i. Allow limited web access and access to isp network services:

Allow limited Web access using HTTP, HTTPS, and FTP, and allows access to ISP network services, such as DNS. Block all other network access. The following access rules will be created:
1. Allow HTTP, HTTPS, FTP from Internal Network and VPN Clients Network to External Network (Internet)
2. Allow DNS from Internal Network and VPN Clients Network to External Network (Internet)
3. Allow all protocols from VPN Clients Network to Internal Network

Rule Name	From	To	Protocol	Network Relation	Users	Action
Local Host Access	Local host	All networks		Route		
VPN Clients to Internal Network	Quarantined VPN Clients, VPN Clients	Internal		Route		
Internet Access	Quarantined VPN Clients, VPN Clients, Internal	External		NAT		
Web Access Only	Internal, VPN Clients	External	Http, Https, Ftp		All	Allow
Allow DNS to Internet	Internal, VPN Clients	External	DNS		All	Allow
VPN Clients to Internal Network	VPN Clients	Internal	All Outbound Traffic		All	Allow
Default Rule	All Networks	All Networks	All Traffic		All	Reject

2.4.3 THREE LEG PERIMETER TEMPLATE:

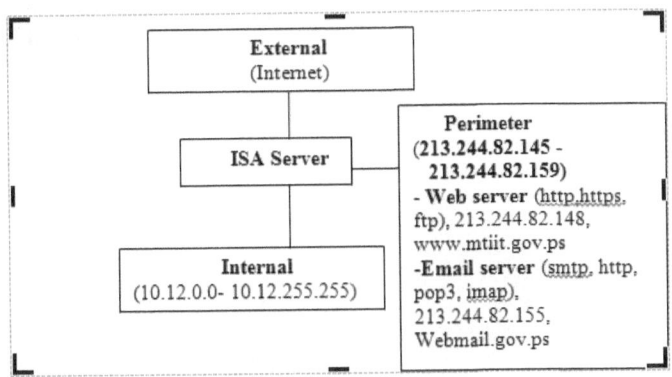

Connect your internal network to internet and protect it from intruders, and publishes services in the perimeter network to internet.

I. Allow limited web access, allow access to network sevices on perimeter network:
Allow limited Web access using HTTP, HTTPS, FTP, only and allow access to network services, such as DNS, on the Perimeter network. All other network access is blocked.
This option is useful when network infrastructure services are available on the Perimeter network. The following access rules will be created:
1. Allow HTTP, HTTPS, FTP from Internal Network and VPN Clients Network to Perimeter Network and External Network (Internet)
2. Allow DNS traffic from Internal Network and VPN Clients Network to Perimeter Network
3. Allow all protocols from VPN Clients Network to Internal Network

Rule Name	From	To	Protocol	Network Relation	Users	Action
Local Host Access	Local host	All networks		Route		
VPN Clients to Internal Network	Quarantined VPN Clients, VPN Clients	Internal		Route		
Internet Access	Quarantined VPN Clients, VPN Clients, Internal	External		NAT		
Perimeter	Quarantined VPN	Perimeter		NAT		

Configuration	Clients, VPN Clients, Internal					
Perimeter Access	Perimeter	External		Route		
Web Access Only	Internal, VPN Clients	External, Perimeter	Ftp, Http, Https		All	Allow
VPN Clients to Internal Network	VPN Clients	Internal	All Outbound Traffic		All	Allow
Allow DNS to perimeter	Internal, VPN Clients	Perimeter	DNS		All	Allow
Default Rule	All Networks	All Networks	All Traffic		All	Reject

2.4.4 FRONT FIREWALL TEMPLATE:

Use the ISA server as front line of defense in a back to back perimeter network configuration. Use this configuration when you have two firewalls between the protected internal network and internet.

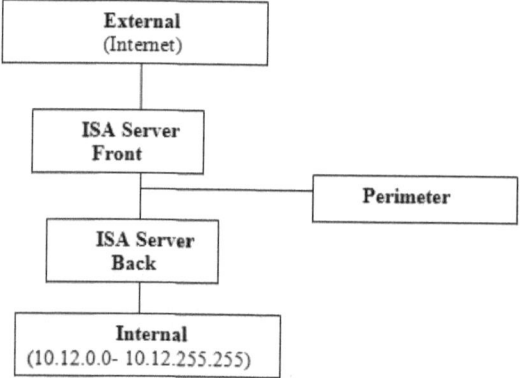

i. Allow limited web access, allow access to network sevices on perimeter network:
Allow access to websites, but no other network access through the firewall. Use this option when you want to allow only Web access. You can modify the policy later to allow other types of network access. This option is useful when network infrastructure services, such as DNS, are available in the Perimeter Network. The following rules will be created:
1. Allow HTTP, HTTPS, FTP from Perimeter Network and VPN Clients Network to External Network(Internet)

2. Allow all protocols from VPN Clients Network to Perimeter Network

Rule Name	From	To	Protocol	Network Relation	Users	Action
Local Host Access	Local host	All networks		Route		
VPN Clients to Internal Network	Quarantined VPN Clients, VPN Clients	Perimeter		Route		
Perimeter Access	Perimeter. Quarantined VPN Clients, VPN Clients	External		Route		
Web Access Only	Perimeter, VPN Clients	External	Ftp, http, Https		all	Allow
VPN to Perimeter	VPN Clients	Perimeter	All Outbound Traffic		all	Allow
Default Rule	All Networks	All Networks	All Traffic		all	Reject

2.4.5 BACK FIREWALL TEMPLATE:

Use the ISA server as the back line of defense in a back-to back perimeter network configuration. Use this option when you have two firewalls between the protected internal network and internet.

I. Allow limited web access, allow access to network sevices on perimeter network:
Allow limited Web access using HTTP, HTTPS, FTP, only and allow access to network services, such as DNS, on the Perimeter network. All other network access is blocked.
This option is useful when network infrastructure services are available on the Perimeter network. The following access rules will be created:
1. Allow HTTP, HTTPS, FTP from Internal Network and VPN Clients Network to Perimeter Network and External Network (Internet)
2. Allow DNS traffic from Internal Network and VPN Clients Network to Perimeter Network
3. Allow all protocols from VPN Clients Network to Internal Network

Rule Name	From	To	Protocol	Network Relation	Users	Action
Local Host Access	Local host	All networks		Route		
VPN Clients to Internal	Quarantined VPN Clients, VPN	Internal		Route		

Network	Clients					
Internet Access	Internal, Quarantined VPN Clients, VPN Clients	External		NAT		
Web Access Only	Internal, VPN Clients	External	Ftp, http, https		All	Allow
Allow DNS to Perimeter	Internal, VPN Clients	Perimeter Address Range	DNS			Allow
VPN Clients to Internal Networks	VPN Clients	Internal	All Outbound Traffic			Allow
Default Rule	All Networks	All Networks	All Traffic		All	Reject

2.4.6 PUBLISHING RULES:

2.4.6.1 WEB SERVER PUBLISHING RULE:

Rule Name	Public Name	From	To (Network Address of the Web server to Publish)	Traffic	Listener	Action
Web server publish rule	Request to www.mtit.gov.ps	Anywhere	Net Address of the server to publish 213.244.82.148	http	External interface: 80	allow

2.4.6.2 SERVER PUBLISHING RULE:

Rule Name	From	To	Traffic	Network	Action
Ftp server publish rule	Anywhere	Net address of the server to publish 213.244.82.148	Ftp	External interface	Allow

2.4.6.3 MAIL SERVER PUBLISHING RULES:

i. Client Access RPC, IMAP4, POP3 SMTP:

Rule Name	From	To	Traffic	Network	Action
SMTP Publish rule	Anywhere	Net sddress of the server to publish 213.244.82.155	SMTP Server	External interface:	Allow
POP3 publish rule	Any where	213.244.82.155	Pop3 Server	External interface	Allow
IMAP4 publish rule	Any where	213.244.82.155	IMAP4 Server	External interface	Allow
Mail Exchange RPC Server	Any where	213.244.82.155	Exchange RPC Server	External interface	Allow

ii. Web Client Access, Outlook Web Access, Outlook Mobile Access, Exchange Server ActiveSync

Rule Name	Public Name	From	To	Protocol	Listner	Action	Path
Web server publish rule	Request to webmail.gov.ps	Anywhere	Net address of the server to publish 213.244.82.155	http	External interface: 80	allow	-/exchange/* -/exchweb/* /OMA/* -/public/* -/Microsoft-Server-ActiveSync/*

iii. Server to Srver Communication

Rule Name	From	To	Traffic	Network	Action
SMTP Publish rule	Anywhere	Net address of the server to publish 213.244.82.155	SMTP Server	External interface	Allow
SMTPS publish rule	Any where	213.244.82.155	SMTPS Server	External interface	Allow
NNTP publish rule	Any where	213.244.82.155	NNTP Server	External interface	Allow

2.4.7 WEB CHAINING:

Rule Name	To	Action	Bridging
Web chaining rule	External	Redirect to specified upstream server, 10.12.0.32 Port:80 SSL: 443	Redirect HTTP request as HTTP request Redirect SSL request as SSL/HTTP request
Default rule	All Networks	Retrieve them directly from specified destination	Redirect HTTP request as HTTP request Redirect SSL request as SSL/HTTP request

2.4.8 CACHING RULE:

There is a default cache rule with default settings, and you can create new ones..

2.5. INTRUSION DETECTION:

By default, the ISA Server is configured with most of the intrusion detection options already enabled. In ISA Server Management, click General, then click Enable Intrusion Detection and DNS Attack detection, then select the attack options that you wish to enable. The attack options: Windows out-of-band attack, Land attack, Ping of death attack, Port scan, IP half scan, UDP bomb, DNS attacks (DNS hostname overflow, DNS length overflow, DNS zone transfer).

2.6. APPLICATION AND WEB FILTERING :

Application and Web filters provide extra layer of security for a network. These filters can examine every packet that flows through the ISA Server and filter the packets based on the results of that inspections.

HTTP filters are applied on a per-rule basis. To configure the HTTP filters on particular access rule or Web publishing rule, modify the HTTP policy for that rule. Right click the rule and choose configure http. You can configure ISA to allow or deny requests based on
- General Properties: ie. Request header, Request Payload, URL protection, Executables.
- HTTP Method: GET, HEAD, POST, PUT, DELETE, TRACE, CONNECT.
- Extensions: configure ISA to allow or deny downloads based on extensions.
- HTTP Headers: Headers contain specific information about the client, including browser and operating system data.
- HTTP Signatures: Block packets based on application signature.

There are also a filters for other types of applications, i.e,
- **DNS filter:** Allows organization to screen incoming DNS communications for malicious commands and data before they reach to DNS server.
- **FTP filter:** Enables FTP protocols (client and server)
- **MMS filter:** Enables Microsoft Media Streaming protocol
- **PNMP filter:** Enables RealNetworks Streaming Media protocol
- **POP intrusion detection filter:** Protects POP email servers from buffer overflow attacks.
- **PPTP filter:** Enables PPTP tunneling through ISA Server
- **PRC filter:** Enables publishing of RPC servers
- **RTSP filter**: Enables Real Time Streaming Protocol
- **H.323 filter:** Enables H.323 protocol
- **Socks version 4 filter:** Enables SOCKS 4 communication
- **SMTP filter:** Uses content inspection to examine SMTP commands and ensure that they are not harmful to organization email. Filters SMTP traffic based on keywords, users/domains, attachments, SMTP commands.

These filters can be enabled and configured from the ISA Server Management/ Configuration/ Add ins, and depend on the application, can be configured from the specific server publishing rule.

3. LINUX SQUID CONFIGURATION

3.1. SETTING UP THE CACHE:

Go to to webmin http://127.0.0.1:10000, then servers, then squid proxy sever, accept the defaults that the cache directory in /var/spool/squid and the user is squid, initialize the cache from webmin.

From the webmin squid server module you can change the caching and proxy options as you wish. I prefer if you increase the size of cache.

3.2. PORTS AND NETWORKING:

By default, Squid listens for proxy requests on TCP port 3128 on all of your system's IP addresses. Because this is not the usual port on which proxies are run (8000 and 8080 seem to be the most common), you may want to change it. If your system has more than one network interface, you might also want to edit the listening address so that only clients on your internal network can connect. To specify the ports that Squid uses, go to Ports and Networking and set the proxy In the first empty field in the Port column, enter a port number like 8000 or 8080. In the Hostname/IP address column, either select All to accept connections on any of your system's interfaces or select the second option to enter an IP address in the adjacent text box. Using this table, Squid can be configured to listen on as many ports as you like. ICP is a protocol used by Squid to communicate with other proxies in a cluster. Fill in the ICP port field to listen on a port other than the default of 3130 for ICP. This is not generally necessary, however, as only other proxies ever use this protocol. Squid will normally accept ICP connections on any IP address. To change this, select the second radio button in the Incoming UDP address field and enter one of your system's interface IPs into its text field. This can be useful if all of the other proxies that your server might want to communicate with are on a single internal LAN.

With my configuration, I set IP address: 10.12.1.149 and the Port:8080

The following procedure made the following changes in the squid config file /etc/squid/squid.conf:
http_port 10.12.1.149:8080
icp_port 3130

3. 3. ACCESS CONTROL LISTS:

An ACL is simply a test hat is applied to a client request to see if it matches or not. Then, based on the ACLs that each request matches, you can choose to block it, prevent caching, force it into a delay pool, or hand it off to another proxy server. Many different types of ACL exist, for example, one type checks a client's IP address, another matches the URL being requested, and others check the destination port, web server hostname, authenticated user, and so on.

Squid has an amazing number of ACL types, although not all are available in all versions of the server. Table lists those that you can create for Squid 2.4 and explains what they do and what the fields on the creation form for an ACL of each type mean.

Type	Purpose	Field
Browser Regexp	Browser Regexp Checks the User-Agent HTTP header sent in the request to identify the type of browser the client system is running. Useful for blocking certain browsers or otherwise treating them differently.	Browser regexp: For entering a Perl-style regular expression against which the browser identification string is matched. For example, IE 5.5 sends the identifier Mozilla/4.0 (compatible; MSIE 5.5; Windows 98; H010818).
Client Address	Checks the IP address of the client making the request against a list of network addresses or IP ranges. Often used to allow only clients from your own LAN.	When you create or edit an ACL of this type, a table with three columns is displayed. Each row in the table defines a matching address range or network, specified either by a starting and ending IP in the From IP and To IP fields, or a network address and netmask in the From IP and Netmask fields. By saving and re-editing a client address ACL, multiple rows may be added to the table.
Client Hostname	Does a reverse DNS lookup of the client's IP address and compares it to a hostname or domain. Also useful for allowing clients within your network.	Domains: A list of host or domain names in which to match clients, such as pc1.foo.com or .example.com.
Client Regexp	Like the Client Hostname ACL type, but tests the reverse address against a series of regular expressions instead.	Regular expressions: A list of Perl-style expressions against which to check the hostname, such as ^.*.foo.com$. If the Ignore case? box is checked, comparisons are done case-insensitively (which is what you always want, as DNS lookups are caseless).
Date and Time	This ACL type matches depending on the current time and day of the week, rather than any attribute of the client or request. Useful for blocking access to your proxy or certain sites during work hours.	Days of the week: If All is chosen, the ACL will match on any day. If Selected is chosen, it will only match on those days selected from the list below. Hours of the day: If All is chosen, the ACL will match at any time. Otherwise, you must enter starting and

			ending times in 24-hour HH:MM format in the adjacent fields. Only requests made within that range will match.
Dest AS Number		AS numbers are used to identify large networks on the Internet. ACLs of this type will match if the destination web server address is within a network with a certain AS number. Not commonly used	AS numbers: A space-separated list of network AS numbers to check to see if the destination address is in it.
Ethernet Address		Matches requests from clients with certain MAC addresses. This can be handy for allowing access from certain systems on a network with dynamic IP addresses, but is useless if there is a router between the clients and the proxy server. This ACL type, however, is only available if Squid is compiled with the --enable-arp-acl option.	Client Ethernet addresses: A list of addresses in the usual colon-eparated format to match, such as 00:D0:B7:1D:FB:A1.
External Auth		When an ACL of this type is in use, clients are forced to log in to the proxy and their usernames are checked against a list.	External auth users: If All users is selected, authentication will be required and any valid user will match the ACL. If Only those listed is chosen instead, only users entered in the text box provided will match. This can be used to give some people access to certain sites while denying everyone else.
External Auth Rexexp		This is like the external auth ACL type, but supports the user of regular expressions against which you can match authenticated usernames.	External auth users: In this text box, you must enter a list of Perlstyle regular expressions against which you can match usernames. If the Ignore case? box is checked, comparisons are done case insensitively.
Maximum Connections		An ACL of this type will match when a single client has more than a specified number of concurrent connections to the proxy server. Useful for cutting down on the load that a client can generate.	Maximum concurrent requests: The number of simultaneous requests above which the ACL matches.
Proxy IP Address		Matches the IP address on the proxy server to which the client is connected. Handy if your system has multiple network interfaces and you want to	IP address: The IP or network address to compare to the local address, such as 192.168.1.100. Netmask: The netmask to apply to the

	treat them differently—for example, by denying connections from the Internet interface.	IP address when matching. If you just want to specify a single IP address, enter 255.255.255.255 here.
Proxy Port	Matches the TCP port on the proxy server to which the client is connected. An ACL of this type might be useful if your proxy listens on multiple ports, one of which is used for transparent proxying	Proxy server port: A space-separated list of port numbers to which you can compare the local port.
RFC931 User	The ident or RFC931 protocol can be used to identify the remote UNIX user connecting to your proxy, assuming that the client system is running UNIX and has the ident daemon enabled. An ACL of this type can be used to allow certain remote users, but is only useful if you control or trust the client systems.	RFC931 users: In this text box, you can enter a list of remote usernames to allow, such as jcameron and fcchan.
Request MIME Type	This type of ACL matches the MIME type used in the client request. The most common ones are application/x-www-formurlencoded for normal POST requests and multipart/formdata for file uploads.	Request MIME type: The type of request that will cause this ACL to match.
Request Method	Every HTTP request includes a method, which is typically one of the following GET Used for normal page requests or form submissions. POST Used only for some formsubmissions. CONNECT Used to open a direct connection to some remote port, typically for SSL. An ACL of this type is often used to block CONNECT requests to non-SSL ports.	The checkboxes selected in this field specify the methods for which the ACL will match.
SNMP Community	This type of ACL is useful only for limiting access to Squid's SNMP agent. You should never need to create one for controlling normal proxy requests.	SNMP community string: The community string that, if used, causes the ACL to match.
Source AS Number	Like the Dest AS Number ACL type, but matches based on the client's	AS numbers: A space-separated list of network AS numbers in which to

		network number instead.	check for the client address.
URL Path Regexp		Matches depending on the path in the requested URL. The path is everything after the hostname and port, such as /images/foo.gif. Useful for detecting requests to pages dynamically generated by CGI programs.	Regular expressions: A list of Perl-style regular expressions against which you can compare the URL path. The ACL is considered to match if any of the expressions do. The comparisons are case-sensitive unless the Ignore case? box is checked.
URL Port		This type of ACL matches depending on the port specified in the requested ACL. Useful for blocking access to non-HTTP ports such as 23 and 25. If no port is specified in the URL, Squid will assume the default for the protocol (80 for HTTP and 21 for FTP).	TCP ports: A space-separated list of ports with which to compare the requested port.
URL Protocol		Matches depending on the protocol specified in the URL—for example, http or ftp. An ACL of this type could be used to block FTP access for some or all clients, or to nonstandard ports.	The boxes checked for this field indicate which protocols the ACL will match. The special cache_object protocol is used only by Squid's cache manager program.
URL Regexp		An ACL of this type matches if the entire requested URL matches any one of a series of regular expressions. Handy for blocking access to certain pages or sites.	Regular expressions: A list of Perl-style expressions against which to check the URL. If the Ignore case? box is checked, comparisons are done case-insensitively—otherwise, they are case sensitive.
Web Server Address		Like the Client Address ACL type, but matches depending on the IP address of the server that the request is for. It can be used to block entire networks or specific systems hosting content that you would prefer your users not to access.	When editing or creating an ACL of this type, a table for entering a series of network addresses and netmasks is displayed. Like all tables in Webmin, it lists all existing networks followed by a blank row for adding a new one. In the first empty field under IP Address, you should enter a network or single IP like 1.2.3.0 or 192.168.1.55. In the adjacent fields under Netmask, you must enter mask like 255.255.255.0 or 255.255.255.255 if specifying just a single address
Web Server		This kind of ACL compares the	Domains: A list of hostnames (like

Hostname	hostname in the requested URL to a list of host or domain names. Because it does not reverse-lookup IP addresses, it is not too useful for blocking access to sites.	www.foo.com) or domain names (like .foo.com) with which to compare the URL hostname.
Web Server Regexp	Like the Web Server Hostname ACL type, but compares the requested hostname with a series of regular expressions instead.	Regular expressions: A list of Perl-style expressions against which you can match the hostname from the requested URL. You should check the Ignore case? box, as hostnames are always case-insensitive.

From the webmin squid module, choose access control list, and create the desired acls. I created the following acls for sake of testing,

Acl name	Type	Includes
Denyed-sites	Web Server Hostname	.msn.com, .webmin.com, .download.com
ftp	URL Protocol	ftp
Internal	Client Address	10.12.0.0-10.12.255.254

There are predefined acls, which includes

Acl name	Type	Includes
All	Client Address	0.0.0.0/0.0.0.0
Localhost	Client Address	127.0.0.1/255.255.255.255
To_localhost	Web Server Address	127.0.0.0/8
SSL_ports	URL Port	443, 563
Safe_ports	URL Port	80
Safe_ports	URL Port	21 (ftp)
Safe_ports	URL Port	80
Safe_ports	URL Port	21 (ftp)
Safe_ports	URL Port	70 (gopher)
Safe_ports	URL Port	210 (wais)
Safe_ports	URL Port	1025-65535 (un registered ports)
Safe_ports	URL Port	80

Safe_ports	URL Port	280 (http-mgmt)
Safe_ports	URL Port	70 (gopher)
Safe_ports	URL Port	591 (file maker)
Safe_ports	URL Port	777 (multiling http)
CONNCECT	Request Method	CONNECT
Manager	URL Protocol	cache_object

Once you have created some ACLs, they can be put into use by creating, editing, and moving around proxy restrictions. Squid will compare every request to all defined restrictions in order, stopping when it finds one that matches. The action set for that restriction then determines if the request is allowed or denied. This processing system, combined with the power of ACLs, allows you to set up some incredibly complex access control rules. To create a proxy restriction, follow these steps:

1. Click on the Access Control icon on the module's main page
2. Click on Add proxy restriction below the list of existing restrictions to go to the creation form.
3. From the Action field, select either Allow or Deny depending on whether or not you want matching requests to be processed.
4. The Match ACLs list can be used to select several ACLs that, if all are matched, will trigger the action. The Don't match ACLs field can also be used to select ACLs that must not match for the action to be triggered. It is perfectly valid to make selections from both lists to indicate that the action should be triggered only if all ACLs on the left match and if those on the right do not. In its default configuration, Squid has an ACL called all that matches all requests. It can be useful for creating restrictions that allow or deny everyone, one of which usually exists by default.
5. Click the Save button to create the new restriction and return to the access control page. Setting Up Proxy Authentication 593
6. Use the arrows next to it in the Proxy restrictions table to move it to the correct location. If your list ends with a Deny all entry, you will need to move it off the bottom for it to have any effect. If the list has an entry that allows all clients from your network and you have just added a restriction to deny access to some sites, you will need to move it above that Allow entry as well for it to be used.
7. When you are done creating and positioning restrictions, hit the Apply Changes link at the top of the page to make them active.

In my case I just created a proxy restriction, that will allow access from the internal network clients, and will prevent access to web servers (denyed-sites: .webmin.com, .msn.com, .download.com), and prevent access to ftp sites. So, I put the action allow, and I set,
Match ACLS: internal acl
Don't match ACL: ftp , denyed-sites acls
Then I moved my ACL up to be above the last default deny all rule.

There are also default acls, so the restriction rule base became,

Restriction Numder	Match	Don't Match	Action
1	manager localhost		Allow
2	Manager		Deny
3		Safe_ports	Deny
4	Localhost		Allow
5	CONNECT	SSL_ports	Deny
6	Internal	Denyed-sites ftp	Allow
7	All		Deny

The above procedure caused the following changes in /etc/squid/squid.conf
acl all src 0.0.0.0/0.0.0.0
acl manager proto cache_object
acl localhost src 127.0.0.1/255.255.255.255
acl to_localhost dst 127.0.0.0/8
acl SSL_ports port 443 563
acl Safe_ports port 80 # http
acl Safe_ports port 21 # ftp
acl Safe_ports port 443 563 # https, snews
acl Safe_ports port 70 # gopher
acl Safe_ports port 210 # wais
acl Safe_ports port 1025-65535 # unregistered ports
acl Safe_ports port 280 # http-mgmt
acl Safe_ports port 488 # gss-http
acl Safe_ports port 591 # filemaker
acl Safe_ports port 777 # multiling http
acl CONNECT method CONNECT
acl internal src 10.12.0.0-10.12.255.254
acl denyed-sites dstdomain .download.com .msn.com .webmin.com
acl ftp proto ftp

http_access allow manager localhost

http_access deny manager
http_access deny !Safe_ports
http_access deny CONNECT !SSL_ports
http_access allow localhost
http_access allow internal !denyed-sites !ftp
http_access deny all

3.4. CONNECTING TO OTHER CACHES:

Instead of retrieving requested web pages directly, Squid can be configured to connect to another proxy server instead and forward some or all requests to it. By making use of ACLs to categorize requests, you can set up Squid to forward only some requests to another proxy while handling the rest normally. For example, your proxy could always handle requests for web pages on your local LAN, but still forward everything else to a master proxy cache system. To set up your server to make use of another proxy for requests except those to a certain network or domain, follow these steps:

1. On the module's main page, click on the Access Control icon.
2. Create a Web Server Hostname or Web Server Address ACL that matches the web servers that your proxy should fetch directly. Call the ACL direct, for example.
3. Go back to the main page and click on the Other Caches icon to bring up a page containing a list of other known proxy servers (if any) and a form for setting options that control when they are used.
4. Click on Add another cache to go to the cache host creation form.
5. In the Hostname field, enter the fully qualified hostname of the master cache server, such as bigproxy.example.com. Do not just enter bigproxy, as Squid sometimes has trouble resolving non-canonical DNS names.
6. From the Type menu, select parent, which tells Squid that this other proxy is at a higher level (and thus has more cached pages) than yours.
7. In the Proxy port field, enter a port number that the other proxy is listening on, such as 8080.
8. In the ICP port field, enter the port that the proxy uses for ICP requests, which will typically be 3130. If you don't know or the master proxy does not support ICP, enter 3130 anyway.
9. Hit the Save button at the bottom of the page to return to the list of other caches.
10. In the form at the bottom of that page is a section entitled ACLs to fetch directly, which is actually an ACL table similar to the Proxy restrictions table explained before Use the Add ACLs to fetch directly link to first add an entry to allow your direct ACL, and then add one to deny the all ACL. This tells Squid to directly fetch pages from local web servers, but pass all other requests on to the chosen proxy.
11. Finally, click on Apply Changes at the top of the page to have Squid start using the other proxy server.

If you just want to have your proxy forward all requests to another proxy server, regardless of their destination, Step 10 in the previous instructions can be skipped completely. This works because Squid will use the other configured proxy by default if no ACLs have been set up to force direct fetching for certain requests.

Squid can be configured to contact other caches in the same cluster for each request, and ask them if they already have the page cached. If so, it is retrieved from the other proxy instead of from the originating web server. Because all the proxies in an organization are typically connected via a fast network, this is far more efficient. The protocol used for this inter-cache communication is called ICP and is only used by Squid.

On the module's main page, click on the Other Caches icon. To set up two or more proxies to talk to each other with ICP, follow these steps on each system:

1. Click on Add another cache to bring up the cache host creation form.
2. In the Hostname field enter the full hostname of one of the other caches.
3. From the Type menu, select sibling, indicating that the other cache is at the same level as this one.
4. In the Proxy port field, enter the HTTP port on which the other proxy listens.
5. In the ICP port field, enter the port number that the other proxy uses for ICP (usually 3130)
6. Hit the Save button to add the other proxy and return to the other caches list.
7. Repeat Steps 2 through 7 for each of the other hosts in the cluster.
8. Finally, click on Apply Changes at the top of the page.

The end result should be that each proxy in the cluster has entries for all the other proxies, so that it knows to contact them for requests not in its own cache. You can, however, set up ACLs to avoid the use of ICP and force the direct fetching of certain requests, just as you can when forwarding requests to a master cache.

I setup my squid server to consider the computer center proxy server 10.12.0.32:80 as a parent server for it, and my configuration caused the following change in /etc/squid/squid.cong

cache_peer 10.12.0.32 parent 80 3130

4. CONCLUSION

The paper talked about basic Microsoft ISA server and Linux Squid Server configuration My conclusion is that, the ISA server can be implemented as a firewall and proxy with wide range of topologies, application filters and intrusion detections. Also the ISA server supports many server publishing scenarios. But implementing the ISA server needs proper topology and configuration of the server, and the firewall clients should be a member of ISA server domain. Squid server can be implemented as proxy server to access http, ftp, gopher and wais sites, although it can block some type of traffics according to the given restriction rules.

5. REFERENCES

[1] http://www,webmin.com web site.
[2] http://www.microsoft.com..
[3] www.squid-cache.org website.

www.ingramcontent.com/pod-product-compliance
Lightning Source LLC
Chambersburg PA
CBHW032312240526
45464CB00023BA/2995